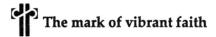 The mark of vibrant faith

Christian Publications
Publishing House of The Christian
and Missionary Alliance
3825 Hartzdale Drive, Camp Hill, PA 17011

92 93 94 95 96   5 4 3 2 1

Please Leave Your Shoes at the Door

Book 5 of the Junior Jaffray Collection of Missionary Stories

Written by Barbara Hibschman

Illustrated by Elynne Chudnovsky
Cover Design by Step One Design
Portrait by Karl Foster
Based on *Please Leave Your Shoes at the Door* by Corrine Sahlberg

CHRISTIAN PUBLICATIONS/Camp Hill, Pennsylvania

CHAPTER 1

Choices

John and Christy Ward sat on the floor of their family room sipping hot chocolate. Their parents were visiting with the Sahlbergs who were missionaries from Thailand.

Even John and Christy's Grandma and Grandpa Ward knew the Sahlbergs and as long as they could remember everyone called them Aunt Corrine and Uncle Elmer. Now, the Sahlbergs were actually in their home.

"It's good to see you again," Uncle Elmer said. "You'll never know how much your prayers and letters have meant to us." The Sahlbergs' picture had been on the Wards' kitchen bulletin board for years. The Ward family had prayed for them often.

"It's been about five years since we've seen you," added Aunt Corrine. "My, how your children have grown!"

"I'm six years old and in the first grade," Christy said.

"And I'm 11 years old and in the sixth grade." John was always glad that he was the oldest.

"The children have been excited about your coming," said mother. "They have lots of questions to ask."

"We'd love to talk to you about Thailand," responded Aunt Corrine. "And we'll try to answer your questions, too."

"Well, Aunt Corrine, I was wondering how come you're a missionary." Christy always had lots of questions.

Aunt Corrine smiled. "That's an interesting story, Christy. As long as I can remember I've wanted to be a missionary. But it really began when I was your age. I went to a children's meeting where I heard about Jesus and how He loved me and died on the cross for my sins. That day I asked the Lord Jesus Christ to come into my heart and forgive me for all the bad things I had ever done.

"Then, one day, a stranger stopped by our house. She was from The Christian and Missionary Alliance church in a nearby town. Her name was Mrs. Clingen. She invited our family of eight children to go to church. My parents didn't go, so Mrs. Clingen made sure that someone came to our house every

Sunday to pick us up and take us to Sunday School.

"Then, when I was 13 years old, I made an important decision."

Aunt Corrine looked at John. "I was just two years older than you are now, John.

"It was missionary conference time at our church. One night, as one of the missionaries spoke, God spoke to me about becoming a missionary. I went to the altar and told Him that I was willing to be a missionary.

"And that's how it all started. Then I went to college and met Uncle Elmer. God chose us to go together to Thailand."

John spoke up.

"I made a choice one Sunday night after church," he said. "I asked Jesus to come into my heart."

"I did, too," added Christy. "Mommy prayed with me."

"You both made the most important choice of your whole life. Just continue to love God by obeying His Word," instructed Aunt Corrine.

John was thinking.

"My dad is like Mrs. Clingen," he said.

"How's that?" asked Aunt Corrine.

"Well, every Sunday he drives the church van and picks up children whose parents don't come to Sunday School and church."

"Maybe some of them will become missionaries like you and Uncle Elmer," suggested Christy.

"You never know," said Aunt Corrine. "The important thing is for us to pray that they make the right choices."

CHAPTER 2

From the Farm Field to the Mission Field

"Uncle Elmer, did you always want to be a missionary, too, like Aunt Corrine?" asked John.

"Oh, no," Uncle Elmer replied. "I always thought I would be a dairy farmer in Minnesota. And then I went into the Army and every-thing changed."

"You joined the Army?" asked Christy. "Weren't you afraid?"

"Yes, I did, and as a matter of fact, I *was* afraid." Uncle Elmer really didn't like to admit that he was afraid. "In fact," he said, "I was so afraid of what might happen to me that I even bought a Bible and started to read it.

"Then, one night, I went to a meeting at the Army chapel. One of the officers came up to me and asked, 'Elmer, are you a Christian?'

"I said, 'I'm trying to be one.' The officer knew right then that I was not a Christian. He saw that I had a

Bible, so he asked me to find John 3:16."

"Oh, that's easy," beamed Christy. "I know John 3:16."

"Can you say it for me?" asked Aunt Corrine.

"Sure. 'For God so loved the world that He gave his one and only son, that whoever believes in him shall not perish, but have eternal life'."

"That's great, Christy," said Uncle Elmer. "You said it without one mistake. I was a soldier in the Army, a grown man, and I didn't even know John 3:16. But the officer explained to me that God loved me and that He sent the Lord Jesus Christ to earth to die for my sins so I could live forever in heaven with Him.

"I prayed and asked Jesus to forgive all my sins. I invited Him to come into my heart. That night He became my Savior and Lord."

"Is that why you are a missionary in Thailand now?"

"I guess that's right, John. But something else happened that made me decide to be a missionary. I started going to a church on a little island way out in the Pacific Ocean. I made some very good friends in that church and it was a sad day when we had to say good-bye to each other."

John looked like he understood what Uncle Elmer was talking about.

"I know what it feels like to move away from your friends. When we moved here, I had to say goodbye to my best friend. His name was Darren. He lived down the street from us."

"Yes," agreed Uncle Elmer. "It's not a happy experience to leave your friends. I remember especially what one man said to me as I shook his hand to say goodbye. He said, 'Won't you come back and help us tell the story of Jesus?' I decided then that I would become a missionary."

"And now you live in Thailand," observed Christy.

"Yes," added Aunt Corrine. "That's where God wants us to be."

CHAPTER 3

Golden Temples and Yellow Robes

"Uncle Elmer, I want to show you the map I made of Thailand." John scooted over beside Uncle Elmer on the sofa.

"Why, John, this is excellent," said Uncle Elmer as he read all the names that John had included on the map. "You have Bangkok, Korat and even the Mekong River marked. Did you make this because we were coming to visit?"

"Well, not exactly. When Mom and Dad said you were coming, I volunteered to do an extra credit report for school. I thought since you would be staying here for a couple of days that I could learn a lot from you about Thailand."

"Me, too," interrupted Christy as she pushed in on the other side of Uncle Elmer. "Do you have something from Thailand that I could take to school for Show and Tell on Friday?"

"Oh, I'm sure we can find something," assured Uncle Elmer. "We

brought a whole suitcase full of interesting things.

"John, while I'm waiting for your Dad to pick me up, why don't we talk about your report?"

"Okay," John beamed. "I have a few questions." Uncle Elmer sat back on the sofa and waited.

"When you first went to Thailand, what did you see that was different from America?"

"Well, one thing we noticed was there were lots of temples with shiny roofs—like gold. We also saw hundreds of monks dressed in yellow robes. Most of the people in Thailand worship an idol called Buddha. His statue can be seen everywhere—in temples, schools, stores and homes."

"What are monks?" asked Christy. She wasn't sure she had heard that word before.

"Monks are men who preach and teach about Buddha. Every morning, after the monks have been to the temple to worship Buddha, they walk down the streets of the city carrying big bowls. They stop at different houses and the people give them rice and other food to eat."

"You mean, they are like beggars?"

"Yes, in a way they are, because they depend on what the people give them to eat. But they do get lots to eat because the people respect them."

"What do the people eat besides rice?" asked John.

"The Thai people like rice and fish. Sometimes they eat something like a soup with vegetables. Their food is very hot and spicy. We learned to eat most of their food, but I never did get used to eating fish for breakfast." Uncle Elmer smiled as the children gasped.

"Fish for breakfast? Yuk! Why didn't you just eat cereal?"

"Cold cereal in boxes is very expensive in Thailand," explained Uncle Elmer. "And besides, we could only buy one kind—Corn Flakes."

"That's it? You mean you couldn't buy Golden Grahams or Cheerios or HoneyCrisp?" Christy thought it was awful that the Sahlbergs could get only one kind of cereal.

"That's right. Last Christmas your parents sent us money for a special treat, so we bought some Corn Flakes. They cost so much that Aunt Corrine and I called them Gold Flakes. But they sure tasted good."

"What are the Thai people like?" asked John. He needed that information for his report.

"Well, the Thai people have brown skin, black hair, and almond-shaped dark brown eyes. They are very polite and respectful and sensitive. We had to learn what to do and not do so we wouldn't hurt their feelings."

"What do you mean, Uncle Elmer?" asked Christy.

"Well, if you lived in Thailand and you went to visit someone, you would have to take your shoes off and leave them at the door. If you went into the house with your shoes on, it would be like walking on someone's bed with your shoes on.

"And, if you lived in one of the villages and I came to eat supper at your house, we would sit on a mat on the floor. The food would be in the center of the mat, and we would eat it with our fingers. You would have to be very careful while you were taking your food out of the bowl that you did not reach in front of someone or over their head. Then you would have to watch that you didn't point your foot at anyone. That would be very bad manners."

"It must have been hard to remember to do everything right. What if you forgot and made a mistake?" asked John.

"Oh, the Thai people know we are from America and that we do things differently here. They are forgiving and understanding. They know that we try to learn their habits and their language.

"Oh, I hear a car horn. Is that your Dad?" asked Uncle Elmer.

"He's here!" announced Christy.

"I have to go now, but we can talk more about Thailand at breakfast tomorrow if you like," said Uncle Elmer as he walked out to the car.

"And I'll make sure you get plenty of Gold Flakes," called Christy.

CHAPTER 4

A Land with No Christmas

"Hey, Mom, the Christmas catalog came today," announced John as he brought the mail into the kitchen and dumped it on the table.

"I wonder if it has a Crimp and Curl doll in it," called Christy from the living room.

"I want to show you and Dad the race car I want," added John.

"Wait a minute, children. We'll have plenty of time to look at the catalog later, but right now I need to start making dinner." Mother turned toward the stove.

"What is a Crimp and Curl doll?" Aunt Corrine asked. Christy picked up the catalog and sat down beside the missionary.

"You can put rollers in her hair and make different hairstyles," explained Christy.

"Oh, that sounds like lots of fun. When we first went to Thailand I would have given anything to have a pretty doll for my daughter

Evelyn. There weren't any dolls like that in Thailand and it cost too much to have one mailed from America."

"So what did you give Evelyn for Christmas?" wondered Christy.

"I made her a doll out of cloth and stuffed it with rice," replied Aunt Corrine.

"Did it look like Raggedy Ann?" asked Christy.

"Well, not exactly, but Evelyn loved her. She took it everywhere.

"They didn't have tricycles in Thailand either. The first time we went we took one with us. As each child got old enough to ride it we painted it a different color. All four of our children used it.

"We also had lots of pets."

"What kind of pets?" Christy wanted to know about the animals. She loved animals.

"At one time we had two dogs, three cats, and four chickens. Also, we had two beautiful horses, two parrots and a little tame deer we called Bambi."

Christy flipped the pages of the catalog still looking for the Crimp and Curl doll.

"Did you have a Christmas tree?" she asked as her eyes scanned the pages.

"Oh, yes. We had a Christmas tree, but it was not a real one. We made it from wire and green crepe paper. And we made our own ornaments from Christmas cards. We also made a manger scene. We turned an old wooden box upside-down. It wasn't very beautiful but it reminded the children, as well as all the visitors who came to our home, that we were celebrating Jesus' birthday. We couldn't buy any special Christmas things because we lived in a country that doesn't celebrate Christmas. There was nothing special in the stores."

"I can't even think of what it would be like not having Christmas," whispered Christy thoughtfully.

"I know it's hard to imagine, but in Thailand there are no Christmas lights or Christmas carols or anything that would remind us of Christmas. Most of the people in Thailand worship Buddha. They don't know or believe in the Lord Jesus Christ. They don't know that we celebrate Christmas because that is when Jesus was born in Bethlehem."

Just then Uncle Elmer walked into the living room.

"Sounds like you're talking about

Christmas."

"Yes, I was telling Christy how we celebrate Christmas in Thailand," answered Aunt Corrine.

"When I think of Christmas, I think about going fishing." Uncle Elmer grinned from ear to ear.

"Fishing? At Christmas time? Isn't it too cold to go fishing at Christmas time?" Christy looked puzzled.

"No. Where we live it is very warm all year. And yes, we really did go fishing at Christmas time. Our four children were home from the missionary kids' school, so our family went to the beach for a vacation. We fished in the ocean. It was so beautiful with its warm, blue water. We also rented paddle boats, played miniature golf and went swimming lots of times. It was so much fun just being together as a family."

"Christy," called Mother from the kitchen. "Please come and set the table."

"You'd better go help your mother," Uncle Elmer said. "I'll tell you about the MK school another time."

CHAPTER 5

MK (Missionary Kid) School

"Mom, we're home," shouted John as he raced up the steps and let the screen door slam behind him.

"Is Uncle Elmer here?" asked Christy. "He promised he would tell us about the MK school."

"Yes, he's here. We're both in the kitchen having coffee. Come and have a snack." Mother pushed her chair over to make room for John and Christy.

"Oh, boy. Oreos and milk!" exclaimed John. Oreos were his favorite snack.

"Is that your school bus down at the corner?" Uncle Elmer asked as he saw the yellow bus pull up at the stop sign.

"Yes, it is. It's a brand new one. Did your kids ride a school bus in Thailand?"

"No, they didn't. In fact, you could never guess how our children got to school. They took a plane!" Uncle Elmer laughed as he saw the expressions on the children's faces.

"You see, our kids went to a boarding school called Dalat. It was in Malaysia, a country a long way from where we lived."

"Your kids took a plane to school?" asked Christy. "You mean they flew back and forth every day in a plane? Was it yellow like the school bus?"

"Oh, no," chuckled Uncle Elmer. "It was a regular passenger plane. They didn't go back and forth every day. They were gone for months at a time. They lived in dormitories with lots of other missionary kids."

"Wow, that would be fun to live with your friends at a boarding school, in a dorm!" John said.

"Well, most of the time it was fun," Uncle Elmer explained. "Each dorm had a dorm mother and father. They helped the kids get their homework done and made sure they got enough time to practice their music lessons. There was lots of time for fun, too."

Christy sat thoughtfully for a moment.

"Uncle Elmer," she asked, "if the kids are away from home for months at a time, don't they get homesick?"

"Yes, we all really miss each other. We write lots of letters back and forth and send pictures. We always pray to God to comfort us. He helps us while we are apart."

"I was homesick at camp last summer," said John. "I even cried at night when I knew no one could see or hear me. I prayed and asked God to help me."

"Yes, God does help us," agreed Uncle Elmer. "God is always with us to help us whether we are at Dalat, or in Thailand, or in the United States, because God is everywhere."

Chapter 6

We're the Team!

"John, how did your soccer practice go today?" asked Uncle Elmer as John puffed through the door.

"Pretty good, I guess. The coach says we have to work harder at being a team."

"That's true," agreed Uncle Elmer. "Team work is important. Everyone needs to work together to make goals and win the game. That's how it is on my team, too."

"Your team? I didn't know you were on a team. What kind of team are you on, Uncle Elmer?"

"Well, it's a team that both your Mom and Dad and your Grandma and Grandpa are on. We are all on the same team."

John and Christy looked surprised. They had never heard of this team.

"You see," explained Uncle Elmer, "Aunt Corrine and I are missionaries in Thailand and we do God's work there. Your mom and dad and your grandparents pray for us. That makes us a team."

"I never thought of it that way,"

said John.

"Oh yes, that's true," added Aunt Corrine. "We always counted on the prayer team here in America. Some people even prayed for us every day. When we faced dangerous situations, we would remember the names of the people who had promised to pray for us. It helped us get through the hard things."

"I remember many times when we were traveling to the villages." Uncle Elmer looked serious. "The roads were very bumpy and sometimes very slippery. Sometimes they were completely covered with water. Other times the road was so bad that we couldn't even ride in the jeep. We had to get out and walk or we used an ox-cart, a bicycle, raft, small boat, pony cart or bus. One time, I even rode an elephant!"

"An elephant?" Christy looked surprised.

"Yes, an elephant! Another missionary and I hired an elephant for a trip into the mountains. It was a very slow ride because every time we came to a stream the elephant filled his trunk with water."

"Oh, no," laughed John. He could already imagine what the

elephant did with the water. "Did he lift his trunk over his back and spray the water?"

"He most certainly did," laughed Uncle Elmer. "He got cooled off and so did we! It was the last and only time we traveled by elephant."

Aunt Corrine leaned forward.

"I remember a trip when there were six people in our jeep. We saw something ahead on the road and thought it was just a small tree. But were we wrong! Instead, the small tree was a snake! A red-hooded cobra snake!"

"A cobra?" exclaimed John. "It must have been really big!"

"Yes, it was so big that the head came up over the driver's door and the tail flipped up to the window on the other side of the jeep. After we ran over it, it just slid away into the jungle."

"Oh, my. I would have been so scared," gasped Christy.

"We were scared, too," admitted Aunt Corrine. "But those kinds of experiences made us thankful for people who prayed for us. God always watched over our family."

Uncle Elmer cleared his throat. He had another story about God's protection.

"One time," he said, "I was in a

bus accident. A big truck coming toward us made the driver swerve. We hit a pothole and the bus went out of control and turned over. I was thrown through the windshield and hit my head on the pavement.

"Dale was traveling with me. He was just nine years old. He got up on the seat of the bus and prayed, 'Don't let my Daddy die!'"

Christy was thinking about what she would feel like if her dad was hurt in an accident.

"I was injured very seriously," Uncle Elmer went on. "The doctors said it was a miracle that I lived.

God answered Dale's prayer and I am here today. So that's what being on a team is all about."

Uncle Elmer looked at John and Christy.

"You know, even children can be part of the missionary team. Every time you pray for a missionary, you're part of the team. Every time you give money for missionary work, you are part of the team."

"Can we be on your team?" Christy asked.

"You sure can. We'd love to have you on our team."

Aunt Corrine smiled and gave Christy a little squeeze.